FATH

DATE:

TODAY I WANT TO SAY TO MY SON

_____

_____

_____

_____

_____

WHAT MY SON DID TODAY AND (WHY) IT MADE ME PROUD/HAPPY/ SURPRISED/UPSET

_____

_____

_____

_____

_____

MY ADVICE TO MY SON

_____

_____

_____

I WANT TO DO WITH MY SON

_____

_____

_____

_____

SON

DATE:

TODAY I WANT TO SAY TO MY DAD

_____

_____

_____

_____

WHAT MY DAD DID TODAY AND (WHY) IT MADE ME PROUD/HAPPY/ SURPRISED/UPSET

_____

_____

_____

_____

MY ADVICE TO MY DAD

_____

_____

I WANT TO DO WITH MY DAD

_____

_____

_____

_____

FATHER

DATE:

TODAY I WANT TO SAY TO MY SON

_____

_____

_____

_____

_____

WHAT MY SON DID TODAY AND (WHY) IT MADE ME PROUD/HAPPY/ SURPRISED/UPSET

_____

_____

_____

_____

_____

_____

MY ADVICE TO MY SON

_____

_____

I WANT TO DO WITH MY SON

_____

_____

_____

_____

SON

DATE:

TODAY I WANT TO SAY TO MY DAD

_____
_____
_____
_____

WHAT MY DAD DID TODAY AND (WHY) IT MADE ME PROUD/HAPPY/ SURPRISED/UPSET

_____
_____
_____
_____
_____

MY ADVICE TO MY DAD

_____
_____

I WANT TO DO WITH MY DAD

_____
_____
_____
_____

FATHER

DATE:

TODAY I WANT TO SAY TO MY SON

_____

_____

_____

_____

_____

WHAT MY SON DID TODAY AND (WHY) IT MADE ME PROUD/HAPPY/ SURPRISED/UPSET

_____

_____

_____

_____

_____

MY ADVICE TO MY SON

_____

_____

_____

I WANT TO DO WITH MY SON

_____

_____

_____

_____

_____

SON

DATE:

TODAY I WANT TO SAY TO MY DAD

_____

_____

_____

_____

WHAT MY DAD DID TODAY AND (WHY) IT MADE ME PROUD/HAPPY/ SURPRISED/UPSET

_____

_____

_____

_____

_____

MY ADVICE TO MY DAD

_____

_____

I WANT TO DO WITH MY DAD

_____

_____

_____

FATHER

DATE:

TODAY I WANT TO SAY TO MY SON

_____

_____

_____

_____

_____

WHAT MY SON DID TODAY AND (WHY) IT MADE ME PROUD/HAPPY/ SURPRISED/UPSET

_____

_____

_____

_____

_____

MY ADVICE TO MY SON

_____

_____

I WANT TO DO WITH MY SON

_____

_____

_____

_____

SON

DATE:

TODAY I WANT TO SAY TO MY DAD

_____

_____

_____

_____

WHAT MY DAD DID TODAY AND (WHY) IT MADE ME PROUD/HAPPY/ SURPRISED/UPSET

_____

_____

_____

_____

_____

MY ADVICE TO MY DAD

_____

_____

I WANT TO DO WITH MY DAD

_____

_____

_____

FATHER

DATE:

TODAY I WANT TO SAY TO MY SON

_____
_____
_____
_____
_____

WHAT MY SON DID TODAY AND (WHY) IT MADE ME PROUD/HAPPY/ SURPRISED/UPSET

_____
_____
_____
_____
_____

MY ADVICE TO MY SON

_____
_____

I WANT TO DO WITH MY SON

_____
_____
_____
_____

SON

TODAY I WANT TO SAY TO MY DAD

_____

_____

_____

_____

WHAT MY DAD DID TODAY AND (WHY) IT MADE ME PROUD/HAPPY/ SURPRISED/UPSET

_____

_____

_____

_____

_____

MY ADVICE TO MY DAD

_____

_____

I WANT TO DO WITH MY DAD

_____

_____

_____

FATHER

DATE:

TODAY I WANT TO SAY TO MY SON

_____

_____

_____

_____

_____

WHAT MY SON DID TODAY AND (WHY) IT MADE ME PROUD/HAPPY/ SURPRISED/UPSET

_____

_____

_____

_____

_____

MY ADVICE TO MY SON

_____

_____

I WANT TO DO WITH MY SON

_____

_____

_____

_____

SON

TODAY I WANT TO SAY TO MY DAD

_____

_____

_____

_____

WHAT MY DAD DID TODAY AND (WHY) IT MADE ME PROUD/HAPPY/ SURPRISED/UPSET

_____

_____

_____

_____

MY ADVICE TO MY DAD

_____

_____

I WANT TO DO WITH MY DAD

_____

_____

_____

_____

FATHER

TODAY I WANT TO SAY TO MY SON

_____

_____

_____

_____

_____

WHAT MY SON DID TODAY AND (WHY) IT MADE ME PROUD/HAPPY/ SURPRISED/UPSET

_____

_____

_____

_____

_____

MY ADVICE TO MY SON

_____

_____

I WANT TO DO WITH MY SON

_____

_____

_____

SON

DATE: _____

TODAY I WANT TO SAY TO MY DAD

_____

_____

_____

_____

WHAT MY DAD DID TODAY AND (WHY) IT MADE ME PROUD/HAPPY/ SURPRISED/UPSET

_____

_____

_____

_____

_____

MY ADVICE TO MY DAD

_____

_____

I WANT TO DO WITH MY DAD

_____

_____

_____

_____

FATHER

DATE:

TODAY I WANT TO SAY TO MY SON

_____

_____

_____

_____

_____

WHAT MY SON DID TODAY AND (WHY) IT MADE ME PROUD/HAPPY/ SURPRISED/UPSET

_____

_____

_____

_____

_____

MY ADVICE TO MY SON

_____

_____

_____

I WANT TO DO WITH MY SON

_____

_____

_____

_____

SON

DATE:

TODAY I WANT TO SAY TO MY DAD

_____
_____
_____
_____
_____

WHAT MY DAD DID TODAY AND (WHY) IT MADE ME PROUD/HAPPY/ SURPRISED/UPSET

_____
_____
_____
_____
_____

MY ADVICE TO MY DAD

_____
_____

I WANT TO DO WITH MY DAD

_____
_____
_____
_____

FATHER

DATE:

TODAY I WANT TO SAY TO MY SON

_____

_____

_____

_____

WHAT MY SON DID TODAY AND (WHY) IT MADE ME PROUD/HAPPY/ SURPRISED/UPSET

_____

_____

_____

_____

_____

MY ADVICE TO MY SON

_____

_____

I WANT TO DO WITH MY SON

_____

_____

_____

_____

SON

DATE:

TODAY I WANT TO SAY TO MY DAD

_____

_____

_____

_____

WHAT MY DAD DID TODAY AND (WHY) IT MADE ME PROUD/HAPPY/ SURPRISED/UPSET

_____

_____

_____

_____

_____

MY ADVICE TO MY DAD

_____

_____

I WANT TO DO WITH MY DAD

_____

_____

_____

FATHER

DATE:

TODAY I WANT TO SAY TO MY SON

_____

_____

_____

_____

_____

WHAT MY SON DID TODAY AND (WHY) IT MADE ME PROUD/HAPPY/ SURPRISED/UPSET

_____

_____

_____

_____

_____

_____

MY ADVICE TO MY SON

_____

_____

_____

I WANT TO DO WITH MY SON

_____

_____

_____

_____

SON

DATE:

TODAY I WANT TO SAY TO MY DAD

_____

_____

_____

_____

WHAT MY DAD DID TODAY AND (WHY) IT MADE ME PROUD/HAPPY/ SURPRISED/UPSET

_____

_____

_____

_____

MY ADVICE TO MY DAD

_____

_____

I WANT TO DO WITH MY DAD

_____

_____

_____

FATHER

DATE:

TODAY I WANT TO SAY TO MY SON

_____
_____
_____
_____
_____

WHAT MY SON DID TODAY AND (WHY) IT MADE ME PROUD/HAPPY/ SURPRISED/UPSET

_____
_____
_____
_____
_____
_____
_____

MY ADVICE TO MY SON

_____
_____
_____

I WANT TO DO WITH MY SON

_____
_____
_____
_____
_____

SON

TODAY I WANT TO SAY TO MY DAD

_____

_____

_____

_____

WHAT MY DAD DID TODAY AND (WHY) IT MADE ME PROUD/HAPPY/ SURPRISED/UPSET

_____

_____

_____

_____

_____

MY ADVICE TO MY DAD

_____

_____

I WANT TO DO WITH MY DAD

_____

_____

_____

_____

FATHER

DATE:

TODAY I WANT TO SAY TO MY SON

_____

_____

_____

_____

_____

WHAT MY SON DID TODAY AND (WHY) IT MADE ME PROUD/HAPPY/ SURPRISED/UPSET

_____

_____

_____

_____

_____

MY ADVICE TO MY SON

_____

_____

_____

I WANT TO DO WITH MY SON

_____

_____

_____

_____

SON

DATE:

TODAY I WANT TO SAY TO MY DAD

_____

_____

_____

_____

WHAT MY DAD DID TODAY AND (WHY) IT MADE ME PROUD/HAPPY/ SURPRISED/UPSET

_____

_____

_____

_____

_____

MY ADVICE TO MY DAD

_____

_____

I WANT TO DO WITH MY DAD

_____

_____

_____

FATHER

DATE:

TODAY I WANT TO SAY TO MY SON

_____

_____

_____

_____

_____

WHAT MY SON DID TODAY AND (WHY) IT MADE ME PROUD/HAPPY/ SURPRISED/UPSET

_____

_____

_____

_____

_____

_____

MY ADVICE TO MY SON

_____

_____

I WANT TO DO WITH MY SON

_____

_____

_____

_____

SON

DATE:

TODAY I WANT TO SAY TO MY DAD

_____

_____

_____

_____

WHAT MY DAD DID TODAY AND (WHY) IT MADE ME PROUD/HAPPY/ SURPRISED/UPSET

_____

_____

_____

_____

MY ADVICE TO MY DAD

_____

_____

I WANT TO DO WITH MY DAD

_____

_____

_____

_____

FATHER

DATE:

TODAY I WANT TO SAY TO MY SON

_____

_____

_____

_____

_____

WHAT MY SON DID TODAY AND (WHY) IT MADE ME PROUD/HAPPY/ SURPRISED/UPSET

_____

_____

_____

_____

_____

_____

MY ADVICE TO MY SON

_____

_____

_____

I WANT TO DO WITH MY SON

_____

_____

_____

_____

SON

DATE:

TODAY I WANT TO SAY TO MY DAD

_____

_____

_____

_____

WHAT MY DAD DID TODAY AND (WHY) IT MADE ME PROUD/HAPPY/ SURPRISED/UPSET

_____

_____

_____

_____

_____

MY ADVICE TO MY DAD

_____

_____

I WANT TO DO WITH MY DAD

_____

_____

_____

_____

FATHER

DATE:

TODAY I WANT TO SAY TO MY SON

_____
_____
_____
_____
_____

WHAT MY SON DID TODAY AND (WHY) IT MADE ME PROUD/HAPPY/ SURPRISED/UPSET

_____
_____
_____
_____
_____
_____

MY ADVICE TO MY SON

_____
_____
_____

I WANT TO DO WITH MY SON

_____
_____
_____
_____

SON

DATE:

TODAY I WANT TO SAY TO MY DAD

_____

_____

_____

_____

WHAT MY DAD DID TODAY AND (WHY) IT MADE ME PROUD/HAPPY/ SURPRISED/UPSET

_____

_____

_____

_____

MY ADVICE TO MY DAD

_____

_____

I WANT TO DO WITH MY DAD

_____

_____

_____

FATHER

DATE:

TODAY I WANT TO SAY TO MY SON

_____
_____
_____
_____
_____

WHAT MY SON DID TODAY AND (WHY) IT MADE ME PROUD/HAPPY/ SURPRISED/UPSET

_____
_____
_____
_____
_____
_____

MY ADVICE TO MY SON

_____
_____

I WANT TO DO WITH MY SON

_____
_____
_____
_____

SON

DATE:

TODAY I WANT TO SAY TO MY DAD

_____

_____

_____

_____

WHAT MY DAD DID TODAY AND (WHY) IT MADE ME PROUD/HAPPY/ SURPRISED/UPSET

_____

_____

_____

_____

MY ADVICE TO MY DAD

_____

_____

I WANT TO DO WITH MY DAD

_____

_____

_____

FATHER

DATE:

TODAY I WANT TO SAY TO MY SON

_____

_____

_____

_____

WHAT MY SON DID TODAY AND (WHY) IT MADE ME PROUD/HAPPY/ SURPRISED/UPSET

_____

_____

_____

_____

_____

MY ADVICE TO MY SON

_____

_____

I WANT TO DO WITH MY SON

_____

_____

_____

_____

SON

TODAY I WANT TO SAY TO MY DAD

_____

_____

_____

_____

WHAT MY DAD DID TODAY AND (WHY) IT MADE ME PROUD/HAPPY/ SURPRISED/UPSET

_____

_____

_____

_____

MY ADVICE TO MY DAD

_____

_____

I WANT TO DO WITH MY DAD

_____

_____

_____

_____

FATHER

DATE:

TODAY I WANT TO SAY TO MY SON

_____

_____

_____

_____

_____

WHAT MY SON DID TODAY AND (WHY) IT MADE ME PROUD/HAPPY/ SURPRISED/UPSET

_____

_____

_____

_____

_____

_____

MY ADVICE TO MY SON

_____

_____

_____

I WANT TO DO WITH MY SON

_____

_____

_____

_____

SON

DATE: _____

TODAY I WANT TO SAY TO MY DAD

_____
_____
_____
_____
_____

WHAT MY DAD DID TODAY AND (WHY) IT MADE ME PROUD/HAPPY/ SURPRISED/UPSET

_____
_____
_____
_____
_____

MY ADVICE TO MY DAD

_____
_____

I WANT TO DO WITH MY DAD

_____
_____
_____
_____

FATHER

DATE:

TODAY I WANT TO SAY TO MY SON

_____
_____
_____
_____
_____

WHAT MY SON DID TODAY AND (WHY) IT MADE ME PROUD/HAPPY/ SURPRISED/UPSET

_____
_____
_____
_____
_____
_____
_____

MY ADVICE TO MY SON

_____
_____

I WANT TO DO WITH MY SON

_____
_____
_____
_____

SON

DATE: _____

TODAY I WANT TO SAY TO MY DAD

_____

_____

_____

_____

WHAT MY DAD DID TODAY AND (WHY) IT MADE ME PROUD/HAPPY/ SURPRISED/UPSET

_____

_____

_____

_____

_____

MY ADVICE TO MY DAD

_____

_____

I WANT TO DO WITH MY DAD

_____

_____

_____

_____

FATHER

DATE:

TODAY I WANT TO SAY TO MY SON

_____
_____
_____
_____
_____

WHAT MY SON DID TODAY AND (WHY) IT MADE ME PROUD/HAPPY/ SURPRISED/UPSET

_____
_____
_____
_____
_____
_____

MY ADVICE TO MY SON

_____
_____
_____

I WANT TO DO WITH MY SON

_____
_____
_____
_____

SON

DATE:

TODAY I WANT TO SAY TO MY DAD

_____

_____

_____

_____

WHAT MY DAD DID TODAY AND (WHY) IT MADE ME PROUD/HAPPY/ SURPRISED/UPSET

_____

_____

_____

_____

MY ADVICE TO MY DAD

_____

_____

I WANT TO DO WITH MY DAD

_____

_____

_____

FATHER

DATE:

TODAY I WANT TO SAY TO MY SON

_____

_____

_____

_____

_____

WHAT MY SON DID TODAY AND (WHY) IT MADE ME PROUD/HAPPY/ SURPRISED/UPSET

_____

_____

_____

_____

_____

MY ADVICE TO MY SON

_____

_____

I WANT TO DO WITH MY SON

_____

_____

_____

SON

DATE:

TODAY I WANT TO SAY TO MY DAD

_____

_____

_____

_____

WHAT MY DAD DID TODAY AND (WHY) IT MADE ME PROUD/HAPPY/ SURPRISED/UPSET

_____

_____

_____

_____

MY ADVICE TO MY DAD

_____

_____

I WANT TO DO WITH MY DAD

_____

_____

_____

FATHER

DATE: _____

TODAY I WANT TO SAY TO MY SON

_____

_____

_____

_____

_____

WHAT MY SON DID TODAY AND (WHY) IT MADE ME PROUD/HAPPY/ SURPRISED/UPSET

_____

_____

_____

_____

_____

_____

MY ADVICE TO MY SON

_____

_____

_____

I WANT TO DO WITH MY SON

_____

_____

_____

_____

SON

TODAY I WANT TO SAY TO MY DAD

_____

_____

_____

_____

WHAT MY DAD DID TODAY AND (WHY) IT MADE ME PROUD/HAPPY/ SURPRISED/UPSET

_____

_____

_____

_____

MY ADVICE TO MY DAD

_____

_____

I WANT TO DO WITH MY DAD

_____

_____

_____

FATHER

DATE:

TODAY I WANT TO SAY TO MY SON

_____
_____
_____
_____

WHAT MY SON DID TODAY AND (WHY) IT MADE ME PROUD/HAPPY/ SURPRISED/UPSET

_____
_____
_____
_____
_____
_____

MY ADVICE TO MY SON

_____
_____

I WANT TO DO WITH MY SON

_____
_____
_____
_____

SON

DATE: _____

TODAY I WANT TO SAY TO MY DAD

_____

_____

_____

_____

WHAT MY DAD DID TODAY AND (WHY) IT MADE ME PROUD/HAPPY/ SURPRISED/UPSET

_____

_____

_____

_____

MY ADVICE TO MY DAD

_____

_____

I WANT TO DO WITH MY DAD

_____

_____

_____

FATHER

DATE:

TODAY I WANT TO SAY TO MY SON

_____
_____
_____
_____
_____

WHAT MY SON DID TODAY AND (WHY) IT MADE ME PROUD/HAPPY/ SURPRISED/UPSET

_____
_____
_____
_____
_____
_____
_____

MY ADVICE TO MY SON

_____
_____

I WANT TO DO WITH MY SON

_____
_____
_____
_____

SON

DATE:

TODAY I WANT TO SAY TO MY DAD

_____

_____

_____

_____

WHAT MY DAD DID TODAY AND (WHY) IT MADE ME PROUD/HAPPY/ SURPRISED/UPSET

_____

_____

_____

_____

_____

MY ADVICE TO MY DAD

_____

_____

I WANT TO DO WITH MY DAD

_____

_____

_____

FATHER

DATE: _____

TODAY I WANT TO SAY TO MY SON
_____
_____
_____
_____
_____

WHAT MY SON DID TODAY AND (WHY) IT MADE ME PROUD/HAPPY/ SURPRISED/UPSET
_____
_____
_____
_____
_____
_____

MY ADVICE TO MY SON
_____
_____
_____

I WANT TO DO WITH MY SON
_____
_____
_____
_____

SON

TODAY I WANT TO SAY TO MY DAD

_____

_____

_____

_____

WHAT MY DAD DID TODAY AND (WHY) IT MADE ME PROUD/HAPPY/ SURPRISED/UPSET

_____

_____

_____

_____

_____

MY ADVICE TO MY DAD

_____

_____

I WANT TO DO WITH MY DAD

_____

_____

_____

_____

FATHER

DATE:

TODAY I WANT TO SAY TO MY SON

_____

_____

_____

_____

_____

WHAT MY SON DID TODAY AND (WHY) IT MADE ME PROUD/HAPPY/ SURPRISED/UPSET

_____

_____

_____

_____

_____

_____

MY ADVICE TO MY SON

_____

_____

I WANT TO DO WITH MY SON

_____

_____

_____

_____

SON

DATE:

TODAY I WANT TO SAY TO MY DAD

_____

_____

_____

_____

WHAT MY DAD DID TODAY AND (WHY) IT MADE ME PROUD/HAPPY/ SURPRISED/UPSET

_____

_____

_____

_____

MY ADVICE TO MY DAD

_____

_____

I WANT TO DO WITH MY DAD

_____

_____

_____

FATHER

DATE:

TODAY I WANT TO SAY TO MY SON

_____

_____

_____

_____

_____

WHAT MY SON DID TODAY AND (WHY) IT MADE ME PROUD/HAPPY/ SURPRISED/UPSET

_____

_____

_____

_____

_____

_____

MY ADVICE TO MY SON

_____

_____

_____

I WANT TO DO WITH MY SON

_____

_____

_____

_____

SON

DATE:

TODAY I WANT TO SAY TO MY DAD

_____

_____

_____

_____

WHAT MY DAD DID TODAY AND (WHY) IT MADE ME PROUD/HAPPY/ SURPRISED/UPSET

_____

_____

_____

_____

MY ADVICE TO MY DAD

_____

_____

I WANT TO DO WITH MY DAD

_____

_____

_____

FATHER

DATE:

TODAY I WANT TO SAY TO MY SON

_____
_____
_____
_____

WHAT MY SON DID TODAY AND (WHY) IT MADE ME PROUD/HAPPY/ SURPRISED/UPSET

_____
_____
_____
_____
_____
_____

MY ADVICE TO MY SON

_____
_____

I WANT TO DO WITH MY SON

_____
_____
_____
_____

SON

DATE:

TODAY I WANT TO SAY TO MY DAD

_____

_____

_____

_____

_____

WHAT MY DAD DID TODAY AND (WHY) IT MADE ME PROUD/HAPPY/ SURPRISED/UPSET

_____

_____

_____

_____

_____

MY ADVICE TO MY DAD

_____

_____

I WANT TO DO WITH MY DAD

_____

_____

_____

_____

FATHER

DATE:

TODAY I WANT TO SAY TO MY SON

_____
_____
_____
_____

WHAT MY SON DID TODAY AND (WHY) IT MADE
ME PROUD/HAPPY/ SURPRISED/UPSET

_____
_____
_____
_____
_____

MY ADVICE TO MY SON

_____
_____

I WANT TO DO WITH MY SON

_____
_____
_____
_____

SON

DATE:

TODAY I WANT TO SAY TO MY DAD

WHAT MY DAD DID TODAY AND (WHY) IT MADE ME PROUD/HAPPY/ SURPRISED/UPSET

MY ADVICE TO MY DAD

I WANT TO DO WITH MY DAD

FATHER

DATE:

TODAY I WANT TO SAY TO MY SON

_____

_____

_____

_____

WHAT MY SON DID TODAY AND (WHY) IT MADE ME PROUD/HAPPY/ SURPRISED/UPSET

_____

_____

_____

_____

_____

_____

MY ADVICE TO MY SON

_____

_____

I WANT TO DO WITH MY SON

_____

_____

_____

_____

SON

DATE:

TODAY I WANT TO SAY TO MY DAD

_____

_____

_____

_____

_____

WHAT MY DAD DID TODAY AND (WHY) IT MADE ME PROUD/HAPPY/ SURPRISED/UPSET

_____

_____

_____

_____

_____

MY ADVICE TO MY DAD

_____

_____

I WANT TO DO WITH MY DAD

_____

_____

_____

_____

FATHER

DATE:

TODAY I WANT TO SAY TO MY SON

_____
_____
_____
_____
_____

WHAT MY SON DID TODAY AND (WHY) IT MADE
ME PROUD/HAPPY/ SURPRISED/UPSET

_____
_____
_____
_____
_____

MY ADVICE TO MY SON

_____
_____

I WANT TO DO WITH MY SON

_____
_____
_____
_____

SON

DATE:

TODAY I WANT TO SAY TO MY DAD

_____
_____
_____
_____

WHAT MY DAD DID TODAY AND (WHY) IT MADE ME PROUD/HAPPY/ SURPRISED/UPSET

_____
_____
_____
_____
_____

MY ADVICE TO MY DAD

_____
_____

I WANT TO DO WITH MY DAD

_____
_____
_____
_____

FATHER

DATE:

TODAY I WANT TO SAY TO MY SON

_____

_____

_____

_____

_____

WHAT MY SON DID TODAY AND (WHY) IT MADE
ME PROUD/HAPPY/ SURPRISED/UPSET

_____

_____

_____

_____

_____

_____

_____

MY ADVICE TO MY SON

_____

_____

I WANT TO DO WITH MY SON

_____

_____

_____

_____

SON

DATE:

TODAY I WANT TO SAY TO MY DAD

_____

_____

_____

_____

WHAT MY DAD DID TODAY AND (WHY) IT MADE ME PROUD/HAPPY/ SURPRISED/UPSET

_____

_____

_____

_____

MY ADVICE TO MY DAD

_____

_____

I WANT TO DO WITH MY DAD

_____

_____

_____

FATHER

DATE:

TODAY I WANT TO SAY TO MY SON

_____

_____

_____

_____

_____

WHAT MY SON DID TODAY AND (WHY) IT MADE
ME PROUD/HAPPY/ SURPRISED/UPSET

_____

_____

_____

_____

_____

_____

MY ADVICE TO MY SON

_____

_____

I WANT TO DO WITH MY SON

_____

_____

_____

_____

SON

DATE: _____

TODAY I WANT TO SAY TO MY DAD

_____

_____

_____

_____

WHAT MY DAD DID TODAY AND (WHY) IT MADE ME PROUD/HAPPY/ SURPRISED/UPSET

_____

_____

_____

_____

MY ADVICE TO MY DAD

_____

_____

I WANT TO DO WITH MY DAD

_____

_____

_____

_____

FATHER

DATE:

TODAY I WANT TO SAY TO MY SON

_____

_____

_____

_____

_____

WHAT MY SON DID TODAY AND (WHY) IT MADE ME PROUD/HAPPY/ SURPRISED/UPSET

_____

_____

_____

_____

_____

_____

MY ADVICE TO MY SON

_____

_____

I WANT TO DO WITH MY SON

_____

_____

_____

_____

SON

DATE:

TODAY I WANT TO SAY TO MY DAD

_____

_____

_____

_____

WHAT MY DAD DID TODAY AND (WHY) IT MADE ME PROUD/HAPPY/ SURPRISED/UPSET

_____

_____

_____

_____

MY ADVICE TO MY DAD

_____

_____

I WANT TO DO WITH MY DAD

_____

_____

_____

FATHER

DATE:

TODAY I WANT TO SAY TO MY SON

_____

_____

_____

_____

WHAT MY SON DID TODAY AND (WHY) IT MADE ME PROUD/HAPPY/ SURPRISED/UPSET

_____

_____

_____

_____

_____

_____

MY ADVICE TO MY SON

_____

_____

I WANT TO DO WITH MY SON

_____

_____

_____

_____

SON

DATE:

TODAY I WANT TO SAY TO MY DAD

_____
_____
_____
_____

WHAT MY DAD DID TODAY AND (WHY) IT MADE ME PROUD/HAPPY/ SURPRISED/UPSET

_____
_____
_____
_____

MY ADVICE TO MY DAD

_____
_____

I WANT TO DO WITH MY DAD

_____
_____
_____
_____

FATHER

DATE:

TODAY I WANT TO SAY TO MY SON

_____

_____

_____

_____

WHAT MY SON DID TODAY AND (WHY) IT MADE
ME PROUD/HAPPY/ SURPRISED/UPSET

_____

_____

_____

_____

_____

MY ADVICE TO MY SON

_____

_____

I WANT TO DO WITH MY SON

_____

_____

_____

_____

SON

DATE:

TODAY I WANT TO SAY TO MY DAD

_____

_____

_____

_____

WHAT MY DAD DID TODAY AND (WHY) IT MADE ME PROUD/HAPPY/ SURPRISED/UPSET

_____

_____

_____

_____

MY ADVICE TO MY DAD

_____

_____

I WANT TO DO WITH MY DAD

_____

_____

_____

FATHER

DATE:

TODAY I WANT TO SAY TO MY SON

_____

_____

_____

_____

_____

WHAT MY SON DID TODAY AND (WHY) IT MADE ME PROUD/HAPPY/ SURPRISED/UPSET

_____

_____

_____

_____

_____

MY ADVICE TO MY SON

_____

_____

I WANT TO DO WITH MY SON

_____

_____

_____

_____

SON

DATE:

TODAY I WANT TO SAY TO MY DAD

_____

_____

_____

_____

WHAT MY DAD DID TODAY AND (WHY) IT MADE ME PROUD/HAPPY/ SURPRISED/UPSET

_____

_____

_____

_____

MY ADVICE TO MY DAD

_____

_____

I WANT TO DO WITH MY DAD

_____

_____

_____

FATHER

DATE:

TODAY I WANT TO SAY TO MY SON

_____

_____

_____

_____

WHAT MY SON DID TODAY AND (WHY) IT MADE ME PROUD/HAPPY/ SURPRISED/UPSET

_____

_____

_____

_____

_____

MY ADVICE TO MY SON

_____

_____

I WANT TO DO WITH MY SON

_____

_____

_____

_____

SON

DATE: _____

TODAY I WANT TO SAY TO MY DAD

_____

_____

_____

_____

WHAT MY DAD DID TODAY AND (WHY) IT MADE ME PROUD/HAPPY/ SURPRISED/UPSET

_____

_____

_____

_____

MY ADVICE TO MY DAD

_____

_____

I WANT TO DO WITH MY DAD

_____

_____

_____

FATHER

DATE:

TODAY I WANT TO SAY TO MY SON

_____

_____

_____

_____

WHAT MY SON DID TODAY AND (WHY) IT MADE ME PROUD/HAPPY/ SURPRISED/UPSET

_____

_____

_____

_____

_____

_____

MY ADVICE TO MY SON

_____

_____

I WANT TO DO WITH MY SON

_____

_____

_____

_____

SON

DATE: _____

TODAY I WANT TO SAY TO MY DAD

_____

_____

_____

_____

WHAT MY DAD DID TODAY AND (WHY) IT MADE ME PROUD/HAPPY/ SURPRISED/UPSET

_____

_____

_____

_____

MY ADVICE TO MY DAD

_____

_____

I WANT TO DO WITH MY DAD

_____

_____

_____

FATHER

DATE:

TODAY I WANT TO SAY TO MY SON

_____

_____

_____

_____

WHAT MY SON DID TODAY AND (WHY) IT MADE ME PROUD/HAPPY/ SURPRISED/UPSET

_____

_____

_____

_____

_____

MY ADVICE TO MY SON

_____

_____

I WANT TO DO WITH MY SON

_____

_____

_____

_____

SON

DATE:

TODAY I WANT TO SAY TO MY DAD

_____

_____

_____

WHAT MY DAD DID TODAY AND (WHY) IT MADE ME PROUD/HAPPY/ SURPRISED/UPSET

_____

_____

_____

_____

MY ADVICE TO MY DAD

_____

_____

I WANT TO DO WITH MY DAD

_____

_____

_____

FATHER

DATE: _____

TODAY I WANT TO SAY TO MY SON

_____

_____

_____

_____

WHAT MY SON DID TODAY AND (WHY) IT MADE ME PROUD/HAPPY/ SURPRISED/UPSET

_____

_____

_____

_____

_____

_____

MY ADVICE TO MY SON

_____

_____

I WANT TO DO WITH MY SON

_____

_____

_____

_____

SON

DATE: _____

TODAY I WANT TO SAY TO MY DAD

_____

_____

_____

_____

WHAT MY DAD DID TODAY AND (WHY) IT MADE ME PROUD/HAPPY/ SURPRISED/UPSET

_____

_____

_____

_____

_____

MY ADVICE TO MY DAD

_____

_____

I WANT TO DO WITH MY DAD

_____

_____

_____

FATHER

DATE:

TODAY I WANT TO SAY TO MY SON

_____

_____

_____

_____

_____

WHAT MY SON DID TODAY AND (WHY) IT MADE ME PROUD/HAPPY/ SURPRISED/UPSET

_____

_____

_____

_____

_____

MY ADVICE TO MY SON

_____

_____

I WANT TO DO WITH MY SON

_____

_____

_____

_____

SON

DATE:

TODAY I WANT TO SAY TO MY DAD

_____

_____

_____

_____

WHAT MY DAD DID TODAY AND (WHY) IT MADE ME PROUD/HAPPY/ SURPRISED/UPSET

_____

_____

_____

_____

_____

MY ADVICE TO MY DAD

_____

_____

I WANT TO DO WITH MY DAD

_____

_____

_____

FATHER

DATE: _____

TODAY I WANT TO SAY TO MY SON

_____

_____

_____

_____

_____

WHAT MY SON DID TODAY AND (WHY) IT MADE ME PROUD/HAPPY/ SURPRISED/UPSET

_____

_____

_____

_____

_____

_____

MY ADVICE TO MY SON

_____

_____

I WANT TO DO WITH MY SON

_____

_____

_____

_____

SON

DATE:

TODAY I WANT TO SAY TO MY DAD

_____

_____

_____

_____

WHAT MY DAD DID TODAY AND (WHY) IT MADE ME PROUD/HAPPY/ SURPRISED/UPSET

_____

_____

_____

_____

MY ADVICE TO MY DAD

_____

_____

I WANT TO DO WITH MY DAD

_____

_____

_____

FATHER

<u>DATE:</u>

TODAY I WANT TO SAY TO MY SON

_____

_____

_____

_____

WHAT MY SON DID TODAY AND (WHY) IT MADE ME PROUD/HAPPY/ SURPRISED/UPSET

_____

_____

_____

_____

_____

MY ADVICE TO MY SON

_____

_____

I WANT TO DO WITH MY SON

_____

_____

_____

_____

SON

DATE:

TODAY I WANT TO SAY TO MY DAD

_____

_____

_____

_____

WHAT MY DAD DID TODAY AND (WHY) IT MADE ME PROUD/HAPPY/ SURPRISED/UPSET

_____

_____

_____

_____

MY ADVICE TO MY DAD

_____

_____

I WANT TO DO WITH MY DAD

_____

_____

_____

FATHER

DATE:

TODAY I WANT TO SAY TO MY SON

_____
_____
_____
_____

WHAT MY SON DID TODAY AND (WHY) IT MADE ME PROUD/HAPPY/ SURPRISED/UPSET

_____
_____
_____
_____
_____
_____

MY ADVICE TO MY SON

_____
_____

I WANT TO DO WITH MY SON

_____
_____
_____
_____

SON

DATE: _____

TODAY I WANT TO SAY TO MY DAD

_____
_____
_____
_____

WHAT MY DAD DID TODAY AND (WHY) IT MADE ME PROUD/HAPPY/ SURPRISED/UPSET

_____
_____
_____
_____

MY ADVICE TO MY DAD

_____
_____

I WANT TO DO WITH MY DAD

_____
_____
_____

FATHER

DATE: _____

TODAY I WANT TO SAY TO MY SON

_____

_____

_____

_____

_____

WHAT MY SON DID TODAY AND (WHY) IT MADE ME PROUD/HAPPY/ SURPRISED/UPSET

_____

_____

_____

_____

_____

_____

MY ADVICE TO MY SON

_____

_____

_____

I WANT TO DO WITH MY SON

_____

_____

_____

_____

SON

DATE:

TODAY I WANT TO SAY TO MY DAD

_____

_____

_____

WHAT MY DAD DID TODAY AND (WHY) IT MADE ME PROUD/HAPPY/ SURPRISED/UPSET

_____

_____

_____

_____

MY ADVICE TO MY DAD

_____

I WANT TO DO WITH MY DAD

_____

_____

_____

FATHER

DATE:

TODAY I WANT TO SAY TO MY SON

_____

_____

_____

_____

_____

WHAT MY SON DID TODAY AND (WHY) IT MADE ME PROUD/HAPPY/ SURPRISED/UPSET

_____

_____

_____

_____

_____

MY ADVICE TO MY SON

_____

_____

I WANT TO DO WITH MY SON

_____

_____

_____

_____

SON

DATE:

TODAY I WANT TO SAY TO MY DAD

_____

_____

_____

_____

WHAT MY DAD DID TODAY AND (WHY) IT MADE ME PROUD/HAPPY/ SURPRISED/UPSET

_____

_____

_____

_____

MY ADVICE TO MY DAD

_____

_____

I WANT TO DO WITH MY DAD

_____

_____

_____

FATHER

DATE:

TODAY I WANT TO SAY TO MY SON

WHAT MY SON DID TODAY AND (WHY) IT MADE
ME PROUD/HAPPY/ SURPRISED/UPSET

MY ADVICE TO MY SON

I WANT TO DO WITH MY SON

SON

DATE: _____

TODAY I WANT TO SAY TO MY DAD

_____
_____
_____
_____

WHAT MY DAD DID TODAY AND (WHY) IT MADE ME PROUD/HAPPY/ SURPRISED/UPSET

_____
_____
_____
_____
_____

MY ADVICE TO MY DAD

_____
_____

I WANT TO DO WITH MY DAD

_____
_____
_____

FATHER

DATE:

TODAY I WANT TO SAY TO MY SON

_____
_____
_____
_____
_____

WHAT MY SON DID TODAY AND (WHY) IT MADE
ME PROUD/HAPPY/ SURPRISED/UPSET

_____
_____
_____
_____
_____

MY ADVICE TO MY SON

_____
_____

I WANT TO DO WITH MY SON

_____
_____
_____
_____

SON

DATE:

TODAY I WANT TO SAY TO MY DAD

_____

_____

_____

_____

WHAT MY DAD DID TODAY AND (WHY) IT MADE ME PROUD/HAPPY/ SURPRISED/UPSET

_____

_____

_____

_____

MY ADVICE TO MY DAD

_____

_____

I WANT TO DO WITH MY DAD

_____

_____

_____

FATHER

DATE:

TODAY I WANT TO SAY TO MY SON

_____

_____

_____

_____

WHAT MY SON DID TODAY AND (WHY) IT MADE ME PROUD/HAPPY/ SURPRISED/UPSET

_____

_____

_____

_____

_____

_____

MY ADVICE TO MY SON

_____

_____

I WANT TO DO WITH MY SON

_____

_____

_____

_____

SON

DATE:

TODAY I WANT TO SAY TO MY DAD

_____

_____

_____

_____

WHAT MY DAD DID TODAY AND (WHY) IT MADE ME PROUD/HAPPY/ SURPRISED/UPSET

_____

_____

_____

_____

MY ADVICE TO MY DAD

_____

_____

I WANT TO DO WITH MY DAD

_____

_____

_____

FATHER

DATE:

TODAY I WANT TO SAY TO MY SON

_____

_____

_____

_____

WHAT MY SON DID TODAY AND (WHY) IT MADE
ME PROUD/HAPPY/ SURPRISED/UPSET

_____

_____

_____

_____

_____

MY ADVICE TO MY SON

_____

_____

I WANT TO DO WITH MY SON

_____

_____

_____

_____

SON

DATE: _____

TODAY I WANT TO SAY TO MY DAD

_____

_____

_____

_____

WHAT MY DAD DID TODAY AND (WHY) IT MADE ME PROUD/HAPPY/ SURPRISED/UPSET

_____

_____

_____

_____

MY ADVICE TO MY DAD

_____

_____

I WANT TO DO WITH MY DAD

_____

_____

_____

FATHER

DATE:

TODAY I WANT TO SAY TO MY SON

_____

_____

_____

_____

WHAT MY SON DID TODAY AND (WHY) IT MADE ME PROUD/HAPPY/ SURPRISED/UPSET

_____

_____

_____

_____

_____

_____

MY ADVICE TO MY SON

_____

_____

_____

I WANT TO DO WITH MY SON

_____

_____

_____

_____

SON

DATE:

TODAY I WANT TO SAY TO MY DAD

_____

_____

_____

_____

WHAT MY DAD DID TODAY AND (WHY) IT MADE ME PROUD/HAPPY/ SURPRISED/UPSET

_____

_____

_____

_____

MY ADVICE TO MY DAD

_____

_____

I WANT TO DO WITH MY DAD

_____

_____

_____

FATHER

DATE:

TODAY I WANT TO SAY TO MY SON

_____

_____

_____

_____

WHAT MY SON DID TODAY AND (WHY) IT MADE ME PROUD/HAPPY/ SURPRISED/UPSET

_____

_____

_____

_____

_____

MY ADVICE TO MY SON

_____

_____

I WANT TO DO WITH MY SON

_____

_____

_____

_____

SON

DATE: _____

TODAY I WANT TO SAY TO MY DAD

_____

_____

_____

_____

WHAT MY DAD DID TODAY AND (WHY) IT MADE ME PROUD/HAPPY/ SURPRISED/UPSET

_____

_____

_____

_____

MY ADVICE TO MY DAD

_____

_____

I WANT TO DO WITH MY DAD

_____

_____

_____

FATHER

DATE:

TODAY I WANT TO SAY TO MY SON

_____

_____

_____

_____

WHAT MY SON DID TODAY AND (WHY) IT MADE ME PROUD/HAPPY/ SURPRISED/UPSET

_____

_____

_____

_____

_____

_____

MY ADVICE TO MY SON

_____

_____

I WANT TO DO WITH MY SON

_____

_____

_____

_____

SON

DATE: _____

TODAY I WANT TO SAY TO MY DAD

_____

_____

_____

_____

WHAT MY DAD DID TODAY AND (WHY) IT MADE ME PROUD/HAPPY/ SURPRISED/UPSET

_____

_____

_____

_____

MY ADVICE TO MY DAD

_____

_____

I WANT TO DO WITH MY DAD

_____

_____

_____

FATHER

DATE:

TODAY I WANT TO SAY TO MY SON

_____

_____

_____

_____

WHAT MY SON DID TODAY AND (WHY) IT MADE ME PROUD/HAPPY/ SURPRISED/UPSET

_____

_____

_____

_____

_____

_____

MY ADVICE TO MY SON

_____

_____

I WANT TO DO WITH MY SON

_____

_____

_____

_____

SON

DATE: _____

TODAY I WANT TO SAY TO MY DAD

_____

_____

_____

_____

WHAT MY DAD DID TODAY AND (WHY) IT MADE ME PROUD/HAPPY/ SURPRISED/UPSET

_____

_____

_____

_____

_____

MY ADVICE TO MY DAD

_____

_____

I WANT TO DO WITH MY DAD

_____

_____

_____

FATHER

DATE:

TODAY I WANT TO SAY TO MY SON

_____

_____

_____

_____

WHAT MY SON DID TODAY AND (WHY) IT MADE
ME PROUD/HAPPY/ SURPRISED/UPSET

_____

_____

_____

_____

_____

MY ADVICE TO MY SON

_____

_____

I WANT TO DO WITH MY SON

_____

_____

_____

_____

SON

DATE: _____

TODAY I WANT TO SAY TO MY DAD

_____
_____
_____
_____

WHAT MY DAD DID TODAY AND (WHY) IT MADE ME PROUD/HAPPY/ SURPRISED/UPSET

_____
_____
_____
_____

MY ADVICE TO MY DAD

_____
_____

I WANT TO DO WITH MY DAD

_____
_____
_____

FATHER

DATE:

TODAY I WANT TO SAY TO MY SON

_____

_____

_____

_____

WHAT MY SON DID TODAY AND (WHY) IT MADE
ME PROUD/HAPPY/ SURPRISED/UPSET

_____

_____

_____

_____

_____

MY ADVICE TO MY SON

_____

_____

I WANT TO DO WITH MY SON

_____

_____

_____

_____

SON

DATE:

TODAY I WANT TO SAY TO MY DAD

_____

_____

_____

_____

WHAT MY DAD DID TODAY AND (WHY) IT MADE ME PROUD/HAPPY/ SURPRISED/UPSET

_____

_____

_____

_____

MY ADVICE TO MY DAD

_____

_____

I WANT TO DO WITH MY DAD

_____

_____

_____

FATHER

DATE:

TODAY I WANT TO SAY TO MY SON

_____

_____

_____

_____

WHAT MY SON DID TODAY AND (WHY) IT MADE ME PROUD/HAPPY/ SURPRISED/UPSET

_____

_____

_____

_____

_____

_____

MY ADVICE TO MY SON

_____

_____

I WANT TO DO WITH MY SON

_____

_____

_____

_____

SON

DATE:

TODAY I WANT TO SAY TO MY DAD

_____

_____

_____

_____

WHAT MY DAD DID TODAY AND (WHY) IT MADE ME PROUD/HAPPY/ SURPRISED/UPSET

_____

_____

_____

_____

MY ADVICE TO MY DAD

_____

_____

I WANT TO DO WITH MY DAD

_____

_____

_____

FATHER

DATE: _____

TODAY I WANT TO SAY TO MY SON

_____

_____

_____

_____

WHAT MY SON DID TODAY AND (WHY) IT MADE ME PROUD/HAPPY/ SURPRISED/UPSET

_____

_____

_____

_____

_____

MY ADVICE TO MY SON

_____

_____

I WANT TO DO WITH MY SON

_____

_____

_____

_____

SON

DATE:

TODAY I WANT TO SAY TO MY DAD

_____

_____

_____

_____

WHAT MY DAD DID TODAY AND (WHY) IT MADE ME PROUD/HAPPY/ SURPRISED/UPSET

_____

_____

_____

_____

MY ADVICE TO MY DAD

_____

_____

I WANT TO DO WITH MY DAD

_____

_____

_____

FATHER

DATE:

TODAY I WANT TO SAY TO MY SON

_____

_____

_____

_____

WHAT MY SON DID TODAY AND (WHY) IT MADE
ME PROUD/HAPPY/ SURPRISED/UPSET

_____

_____

_____

_____

_____

MY ADVICE TO MY SON

_____

_____

I WANT TO DO WITH MY SON

_____

_____

_____

_____

SON

DATE:

TODAY I WANT TO SAY TO MY DAD

_____

_____

_____

_____

WHAT MY DAD DID TODAY AND (WHY) IT MADE ME PROUD/HAPPY/ SURPRISED/UPSET

_____

_____

_____

_____

_____

MY ADVICE TO MY DAD

_____

_____

I WANT TO DO WITH MY DAD

_____

_____

_____

Made in the USA
Coppell, TX
28 December 2023

26982133R00068